You and Me

We Can Be Friends

Denise M. Jordan

Heinemann Library
Chicago, Illinois

Customer Service 888-454-2279
Visit our website at www.heinemannlibrary.com

Designed by Sue Emerson, Heinemann Library; Page layout by Que-Net Media™
Printed and bound in China by South China Printing Company Limited
Photo research by Janet Lankford Moran

08 07 06 05 04
10 9 8 7 6 5 4 3 2 1

Library of Congress Cataloging-in-Publication Data
Jordan, Denise.
  We can be friends / Denise M. Jordan.
      p. cm. – (You and me)
Summary: Simple text and pictures explain how, why, where, and when of sharing friendship.
  ISBN 1-4034-4407-2 (HC), ISBN 1-4034-4413-7 (Pbk.)
  1. Friendship in children–Juvenile literature. [1. Friendship.] I. Title.
  BF723.F68J67 2003
  177'.62–dc22

                                       2003012849

Acknowledgments
The author and publishers are grateful to the following for permission to reproduce copyright material:
p. 4 Dennis Degnan/Corbis; pp. 5, 12 Que-Net/Heinemann Library; p. 6 David Young-Wolff/PhotoEdit Inc.; p. 7 Norbert Schaefer/Corbis; p. 8 Spencer Grant/PhotoEdit Inc.; pp. 9, 17 Getty Images; pp. 10, 22, 24 Warling Studios/Heinemann Library; p. 11 Richard Lord/PhotoEdit Inc.; p. 13 Gary Conner/PhotoEdit Inc.; p. 14 Frank Siteman/PhotoEdit Inc.; pp. 15, 19 Laura Dwight/Corbis; p. 16 Felicia Martinez/PhotoEdit Inc.; p. 18 Tom & Dee Ann McCarthy/Corbis; p. 20 Robert Lifson/Heinemann Library; p. 21 Corbis; p. 23 (T-B) Spencer Grant/PhotoEdit Inc., Que-Net/Heinemann Library; back cover Que-Net/Heinemann Library

Cover photograph by Getty Images

Every effort has been made to contact copyright holders of any material reproduced in this book.
Any omissions will be rectified in subsequent printings if notice is given to the publisher.

Special thanks to our advisory panel for their help in the preparation of this book:

Alice Bethke, Library Consultant
Palo Alto, CA

Eileen Day, Preschool Teacher
Chicago, IL

Kathleen Gilbert,
Second Grade Teacher
Round Rock, TX

Sandra Gilbert,
Library Media Specialist
Fiest Elementary School
Houston, TX

Jan Gobeille,
Kindergarten Teacher
Garfield Elementary
Oakland, CA

Angela Leeper,
Educational Consultant
Wake Forest, NC

Some words are shown in bold, **like this.**
You can find them in the picture glossary on page 23.

Contents

What Is a Friend?

A friend is someone you like.

You enjoy being with a friend.

Some friends are old friends.

You can make new friends, too.

Where Can You Find Friends?

You can find friends at school.

You can find friends in your classroom.

You can find friends at the park, too.

You can find friends in many different places.

Why Do You Need Friends?

You can share **secrets** or good news with a friend.

You can play games with a friend, too.

A friend can teach you
something new.

It is good to have a friend.

Who Can Be a Friend?

You can be friends with a classmate.

You and your classmate can eat lunch together at school.

You can be friends with adults
in your community, too.

What Do You See When You Make Friends?

You may see friends **shaking hands.**

Others may be smiling and talking.

You may see friends playing together.

They may be on the same soccer team!

What Do You Hear When You Make Friends?

You hear people say "hello" when they meet someone new.

You hear them tell their names.

You hear questions like "What do you like to do?"

You may hear that you like to do the same things!

What Do Friends Do?

Some friends play together.

Some friends work together, too.

Friends cheer you up when you are sad.

A friend can make you smile.

How Do Friends Act?

Friends are kind to each other.

Friends are helpful, too.

Friends are nice to each other.

Friends are always willing to share with each other.

How Do You Feel When You Make Friends?

It is fun to have someone to laugh and talk with.

It feels nice to do fun things with your friends.

It's nice to have someone to share your time with.

It feels good to make friends.

Quiz

How can you make friends?

Look for the answer on page 24.

Picture Glossary

secret
page 8

shaking hands
page 12

Note to Parents and Teachers

Reading for information is an important part of a child's literacy development. Learning begins with a question about something. Help children think of themselves as investigators and researchers by encouraging their questions about the world around them. Each chapter in this book begins with a question. Read the question together. Look at the pictures. Talk about what you think the answer might be. Then read the text to find out if your predictions were correct. Think of other questions you could ask about the topic, and discuss where you might find the answers.

Index

Answer to quiz on page 22

Ask if you can play, too!